BENJAMIN BRITTEN

MEDIUM/LOW VOICE

12 SELECTED FOLKSONG ARRANGEMENTS

Edited by Richard Walters

Also Available:
BENJAMIN BRITTEN
COMPLETE FOLKSONG ARRANGEMENTS
High Voice
Medium/Low Voice

To access companion recorded performances and accompaniments online, visit:
www.halleonard.com/mylibrary

2534-7916-3003-6732

BOOSEY & HAWKES

DISTRIBUTED BY
HAL•LEONARD®
CORPORATION
7777 W. BLUEMOUND RD. P.O. BOX 13819 MILWAUKEE, WI 53213

www.boosey.com
www.halleonard.com

CONTENTS

Performers on the Recordings: [1] **Kathleen Sonnentag, mezzo-soprano**
[2] **Kurt Ollmann, baritone**
Richard Walters, piano

The price of this publication includes access to companion recorded performances and accompaniments online, for download or streaming, using the unique code found on the title page. Visit **www.halleonard.com/mylibrary** and enter the access code.

NOTES ON THE SONGS

A principal source for much of the information in this section:
Benjamin Britten: A Catalogue of the Published Works,
compiled and edited by Paul Banks,
published by The Britten-Pears Library for the Britten Estate Limited

Songs from VOLUME 1: BRITISH ISLES

Arrangements composed October 1941 (?), 1942. High Voice (original) published by Boosey & Hawkes, 1943. Medium Voice transposed edition published by Boosey & Hawkes, 1946.

The Ash Grove

First known performance: Peter Pears, tenor, Benjamin Britten, piano, 14 December 1941, Southold High School, Long Island, New York.

Dedicated to Beata Mayer, one of the young adult children in the Mayer family, who reportedly nursed him in illness.

The Salley Gardens

Text by William Butler Yeats. The tune is "The Maids of Mourne Shorne." Published source for the melody: *The Complete Collection of Irish Music*, collected by George Petrie, edited by C.V. Stanford. First known performance: Peter Pears, tenor, Benjamin Britten, piano, 26 November 1941, First (Park) Congregational Church, Grand Rapids, Michigan. Britten transcribed this setting for high voice and string orchestra, first performed by Peter Pears and the New London Orchestra, Alex Sherman, conductor, 13 December 1942, London. Britten also created a version for voice and fuller orchestra in 1955. Both orchestrated versions are included in the study score *Fourteen Folksongs Arranged for Voice and Orchestra* (Boosey & Hawkes); performance materials are available on rental from Boosey & Hawkes. Britten also adapted his arrangement for unison voices and piano.

Dedicated to Clytie Mundy, a voice teacher in New York with whom Peter Pears made remarkable progress.

Songs from VOLUME 3: BRITISH ISLES

Arrangements composed from sometime in 1945 to October, 1946. High Voice (original) published by Boosey & Hawkes, 1948. Medium Voice transposed edition published by Boosey & Hawkes, 1948.

Dedicated to Joan Cross (1900-1993), British soprano, original performer of several Britten opera roles: Ellen Orford in *Peter Grimes*, Lady Billows in *Albert Herring*, Female Chorus in *The Rape of Lucretia*, Elizabeth in *Gloriana*, Mrs. Grose in *The Turn of the Screw*.

Come you not from Newcastle?

First known performance: Joan Cross, soprano, Nina Milkina, piano, 21 February 1946, BBC Light Programme. Britten orchestrated the arrangement c. 1959; first performance is not known. The orchestrated version is included in the study score *Fourteen Folksongs Arranged for Voice and Orchestra* (Boosey & Hawkes); performance materials are available on rental from Boosey & Hawkes.

O Waly, Waly

First known performance: Peter Pears, tenor, Benjamin Britten, piano, 31 October 1946, Kleine Zaal, Concertgebouw, Amsterdam. The date of Britten's orchestrated version is not known, nor is its first performance. The orchestrated version is included in the study score *Fourteen Folksongs Arranged for Voice and Orchestra* (Boosey & Hawkes); performance materials are available on rental from Boosey & Hawkes.

Sweet Polly Oliver

First known performance: Peter Pears, tenor, Benjamin Britten, piano, 26 September 1945, Grammar School, Bristol, England.

There's none to soothe

First known performance: Peter Pears, tenor, Benjamin Britten, piano, 27 September 1945, Melksham Music Club, Melksham House, Melksham, England.

Songs from VOLUME 4: MOORE'S IRISH MELODIES

Arrangements composed 1957. High Voice (original) published by Boosey & Hawkes, 1960.

This note from Britten appeared in the original publication:

All the texts of these songs are from Thomas Moore's *Irish Melodies*, published between 1808 and 1834—in one case from the slightly later *National Melodies*. In most instances I have also taken the tunes from the same sources (music arranged by Sir John Stevenson); however, in a few cases I have preferred to go back to Bunting's *Ancient Music of Ireland*, which had in the first place inspired Tom Moore to write his lyrics.

Dedicated to Anthony Gishford, a longtime friend and an employee at Boosey & Hawkes who organized Britten's business affairs.

At the mid hour of night

Original tune to which Moore set his words: "Molly, my Dear." First performance: not known.

Sail on, sail on

Original tune to which Moore set his words: "The Humming of the Ban." First performance: not known.

Songs from VOLUME 5: BRITISH ISLES

Arrangements composed 1951-59. High Voice (original) published by Boosey & Hawkes, 1961.

The Brisk Young Widow

First known performance: Peter Pears, tenor, Benjamin Britten, piano, 24 January 1954, Victoria and Albert Museum, London.

Early one morning

First known performance: Peter Pears, tenor, Benjamin Britten, piano, 23 April 1957, Mozartsaal, Konzerthaus, Vienna. Britten also used this song (in a different setting) in the score for the 1936 documentary film *Village Harvest*.

Song from VOLUME 6: ENGLAND

Arrangements, for high voice and guitar, composed from sometime in 1956 to October 1958 (?). Published by Boosey & Hawkes, 1961. Guitar part edited by Julian Bream.

The editor made a transcription for voice and piano for *Benjamin Britten: Complete Folksong Arrangements*, the source for this collection.

I will give my love an apple

First known performance: Peter Pears, tenor, Julian Bream, guitar, 6 May 1956, Wigmore Hall, London.

Song from TOM BOWLING AND OTHER SONG ARRANGEMENTS

This volume of various song arrangements, previously unpublished, was released by Boosey & Hawkes, 2001. The title of the collection was given by the publisher.

Greensleeves

Arrangement composed 1941(?). This famous English tune, dating back, first mentioned in the "Stationers' Register" 1580, has had various versions. Britten's source is unknown. First performance: not known.

To Beata Mayer

The Ash Grove

Welsh Tune

original key: A♭ Major

Arranged by
BENJAMIN BRITTEN

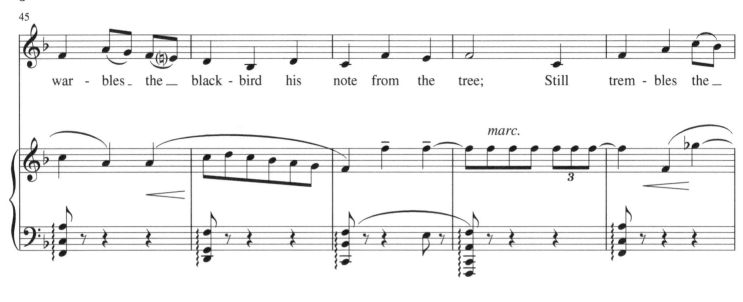

war - bles_ the_ black - bird his note from the tree; Still trem - bles the_

moon - beam on stream - let__ and_ foun - tain, But what are_ the_ beau - ties of

na - ture to me. With sor - row,_ deep_ sor - row, my bos - om_ is_

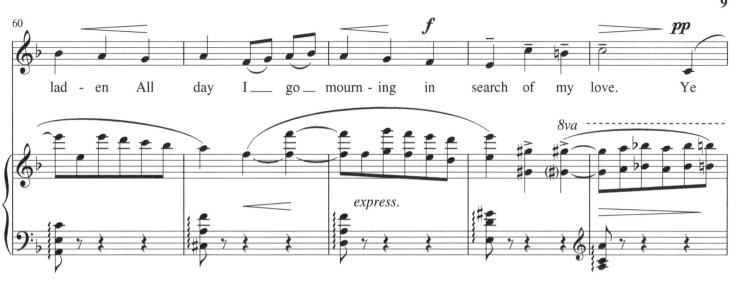

lad - en All day I__ go__ mourn - ing in search of my love. Ye

express.

ech - oes, O tell me, where is the__ sweet__ maid - en? She sleeps 'neath the__

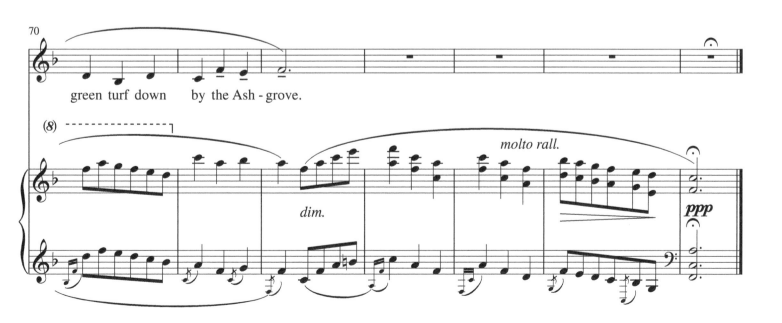

green turf down by the Ash - grove.

molto rall.

dim.

At the mid hour of night

(*Molly, my Dear*)

original key: E♭ Major

from Thomas Moore's *Irish Melodies*

Arranged by
BENJAMIN BRITTEN

Ped. to the end

The Brisk Young Widow

original key: D Major

*Words and Melody
collected by CECIL SHARP

Arranged by
BENJAMIN BRITTEN

Brisk

always stacc.

1. In Ches-ter town there liv'd   A brisk young wid-ow,   For beau-ty and fine
3. Says she: I'm not for you   Nor no such fel-low,   I'm for a live-ly

clothes   None could ex-cel her,   She was prop-er stout and tall,   Her
lad   With lands and rich-es,   'Tis _ not your hogs and yowes   Can

fin-gers long and small,   She's a come-ly dame with-all,   She's a brisk young wid-ow.
main-tain fur-be-lows,   My _ silk and sat-in clothes   Are _ all my glo-ry.

Copyright in U.S.A. 1958 by Boosey & Co. Ltd.
© under U.C.C. 1961 by Boosey & Co. Ltd.
New transposition © 2006 by Boosey & Hawkes Music Publishers Ltd

2. A
4. O

lov - er soon there came,   A   brisk young farm - er,   With his hat turn'd up all
mad - am, don't be   coy   For   all your glo - ry,   For __ fear of an - o - ther

mf

(heavy)

round,   Seek - ing to gain her.   My __ dear, for love of   you   This
day   And an - o - ther sto - ry.   If the world on you should frown   Your

wide world I'd   go through   If __ you will but prove true   You shall wed   a farm - er.
top - knot must come down   To a Lind - sey - wool - sey gown.   Where is then your glo - ry?

f

5. At last there came that way A soot-y col-lier, With his hat bent down all round, He soon did gain her: Where-at the farm-er swore; "The wid-ow's mazed, I'm sure. I'll _ nev-er court no more A _ brisk young wid-ow!"

with Ped.

Come you not from Newcastle?

Hullah's Song Book (English)

original key: F Major

Arranged by
BENJAMIN BRITTEN

O Waly, Waly

from Somerset (Cecil Sharp) *
original key: A Major

Arranged by
BENJAMIN BRITTEN

SHELVING
8/9/2024

Qty: 1

Location:
70-01-008-01-_

Customer PO #:
ETZ09488100

Title:
Benjamin Britten 12 Selected Folksong Arra
ngements

O, love is hand - some and love is fine, and love's a

jew - el while it is new, But when it is old, it grow - eth

cold, and fades a - way like morn - ing dew.

Early one morning

original key: G♭ Major

Arranged by
BENJAMIN BRITTEN

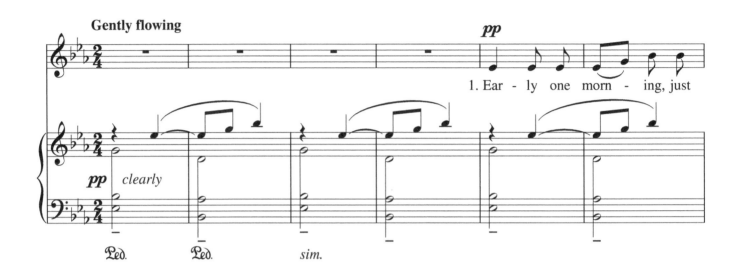

1. Ear - ly one morn - ing, just

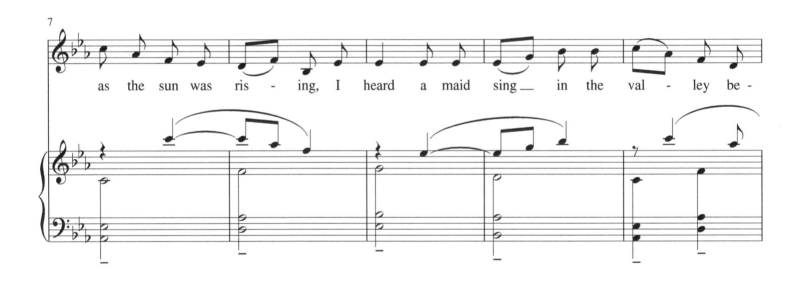

as the sun was ris - ing, I heard a maid sing ___ in the val - ley be -

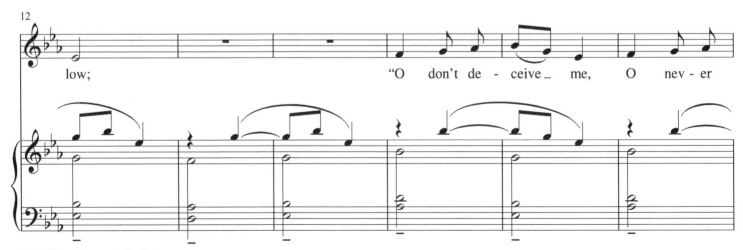

low; "O don't de - ceive ___ me, O nev - er

more expressive

poor _ maid-en so?   3. Re - mem - ber the vows _ that you

more expressive

made _ to your Ma - ry, Re - mem - ber the bow'r _ where you vow'd _ to be true;

cresc.

O don't de - ceive _ me, O nev - er leave _ me!

How _ could you use _ a _ poor _ maid-en so?"

dim.

very quietly

4. Thus sung the poor maid - en, her sor - row be - wail - ing, Thus

sung the poor maid _ in the val - ley be - low;

"O don't de - ceive _ me! O do not leave _ me! How _ could you use _ a _

poor _ maid - en so?"

Ped.   *

Greensleeves

Traditional Folk Song

original key: G minor

Arranged by
BENJAMIN BRITTEN

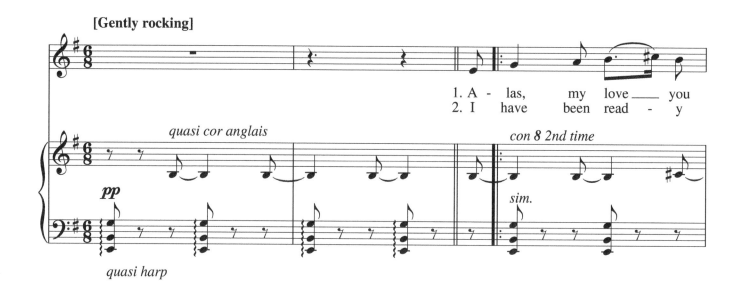

[Gently rocking]

quasi cor anglais

con 8 2nd time

pp

sim.

quasi harp

1. A - las, my love ___ you
2. I have been read - y

do me wrong ___ To cast me off ___ dis - cour - teous - ly; And
at your hand ___ To grant me what ev - er you did crave; And

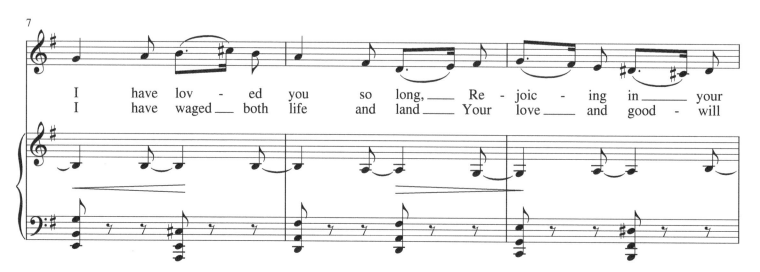

I have lov - ed you so long, ___ Re - joic - ing in ___ your
I have waged ___ both life and land ___ Your love ___ and good - will

I will give my love an apple

original key: A minor

*Words and Melody from
"Folk Songs for Schools"
collected and arranged by
H. E. D. HAMMOND and R. VAUGHAN WILLIAMS

Folk Song from Dorset
Arranged for voice and guitar by
BENJAMIN BRITTEN
Transcribed for piano by
Richard Walters

By permission of Novello & Co. Ltd.

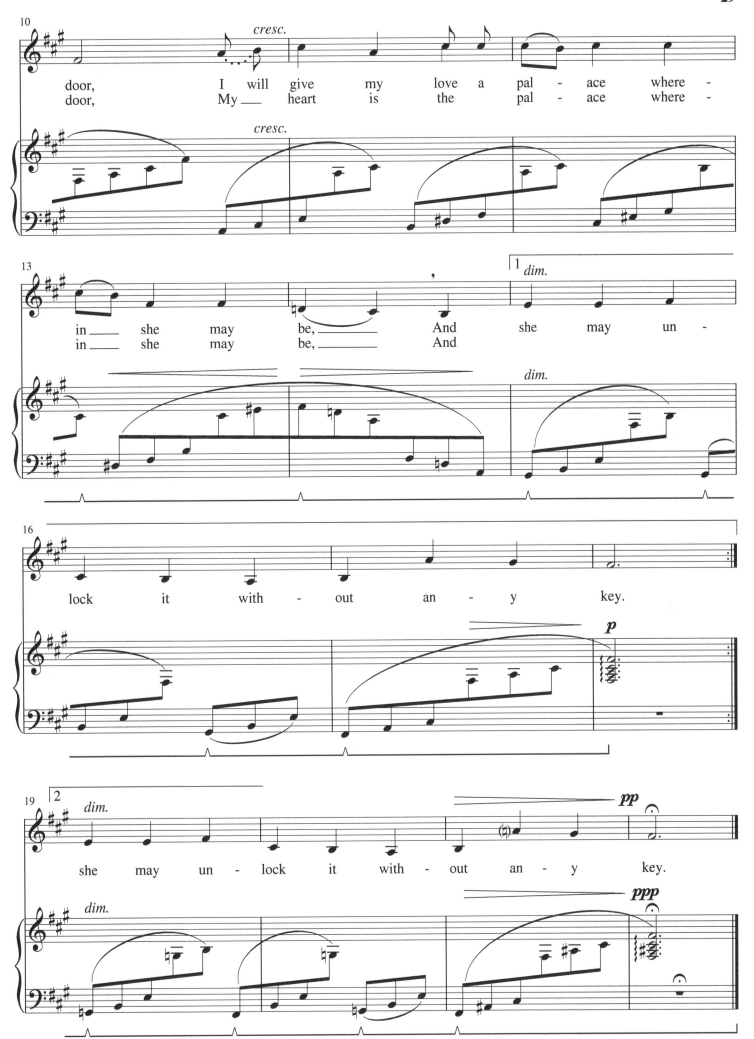

Sail on, sail on
(*The Humming of the Ban*)
original key: F Major

from Thomas Moore's *Irish Melodies*

Arranged by
BENJAMIN BRITTEN

Quietly rocking

p

1. Sail on, sail on, thou
2. Sail on, sail on, through

p
very smooth

with Ped.

pp　　　　　　　　　　　　　*cresc.*

fear-less bark, Wher-ev-er blows the wel-come wind; It can-not lead to
end-less space, Through calm, through tem-pest, stop no more; The storm-iest sea's a

pp　　　　　*cresc.*

scenes more dark, More sad than those we leave be-hind. Each
rest-ing place To him who leaves such hearts on shore. Or,

più f

To Clytie Mundy

The Salley Gardens

Irish Tune

original key: G♭ Major

*Words by
W. B. YEATS

Arranged by
BENJAMIN BRITTEN

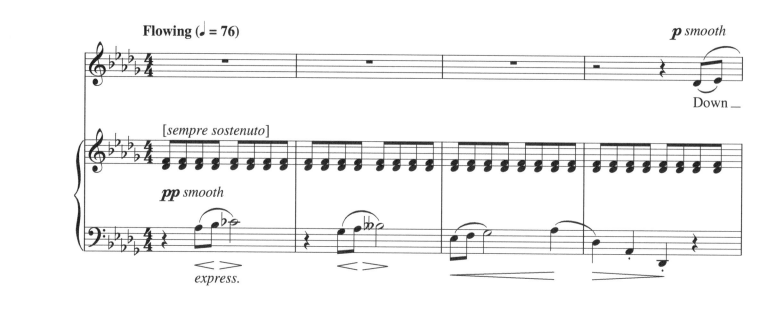

Sweet Polly Oliver

Old English Tune

original key: E Major

Arranged by
BENJAMIN BRITTEN

love." So ear-ly next morn-ing she

soft-ly a - rose, And dressed her-self up __ in her __ dead broth-er's

clothes. She cut __ her hair close, and __ she __ stained her face brown, And

went for a sol - dier to fair __ Lon - don Town.

Then up spoke the ser - geant one day __ at his drill. "Now who's good for nurs - ing? A __ cap - tain, he's ill." "I'm read - y," said Pol - ly __ To __ nurse him she's gone, And finds it's her true __ love all wast - ed and wan.

The first week the doc-tor kept shak-ing his head, "No nurs-ing, young fel-low, can __ save him," he said. But when __ Pol-ly Ol-i-ver __ had __ nursed him back to life He cried, "You have cher-ished him as

There's none to soothe

Hullah's Song Book (Scottish)

original key: D♭ Major

Arranged by
BENJAMIN BRITTEN